Whatever is true, whatever is noble, whatever is right, whatever is pure, whatever is lovely, whatever is admirable—if anything is excellent or praiseworthy—think about such things.

— Philippians 4:8

Good News for a Month

Recognizing What Matters Most

J. Arthur Teresi

To my Lord and Savior,
the One who said, "Because I live, you also will live." (John 14:19)

Contents

Where to Begin
(Laying the Foundation)

Eternal Thanks
(Recognizing Your Blessings)

Trials & Triumphs
(Acknowledging & Overcoming Obstacles)

At the Heart of It All
(Receiving Christ)

Life in Christ
(Committing Your Life to Christ)

Characteristics of Christ
(Living in His Likeness)

Where to Go from Here
(Finishing the Race)

A Note from the Author

As its subtitle suggests, this book is about *Recognizing What Matters Most*, namely, your relationship with God. It's the culmination of years of creative writing I have devoted to Him. It really is *Good News for a Month.*

Each day begins with a Bible verse followed by an inspirational "cubed" poem—which I will talk more about on the next page—three thought provoking questions, an action step, and a bit of good news. Each day is designed to shed new light on the Word of God and provide practical ways to apply it to your life.

No matter where you are in your spiritual journey, whether you are full of doubt or someone with unmovable faith, this book is for you. It covers such issues as overcoming addiction, battling depression, and dealing with adversity; to loving your neighbor, strengthening your faith, living a life of integrity, and experiencing the best day ever. Other topics we will visit include: hope, the Good News, forgiveness, and the meaning of life.

The goal of this book is to get you thinking about God's Word *daily.* If you don't currently read the Bible daily, think of it as a springboard or steppingstone to doing so. If you already do, it's a great supplement.

By no means do I claim to be an expert when it comes to Scripture (I have a degree in business, not theology). However, I do study the Bible every day and pray regularly for revelation. God has given me a gift I know I need to share with the world. A gift I feel has drawn and continues to draw me closer and closer to Him. A gift I feel can do the same for you.

Psalm 96:1 says, "Sing to the Lord a new song." This book is my song.

What Is "Cubed" Poetry?

"Cubed" poetry has two rules:

1. Each pair of lines must rhyme.
2. The number of spoken syllables in each line must equal the total number of lines.

Example:

If the poem has 14 spoken syllables in the first line, there must be 14 spoken syllables in every line, and there must be a total of 14 lines.

Question:

How does that make it "cubed"? How does having 14 lines and 14 spoken syllables per line make the poem "cubed"? Wouldn't that just make it squared (14x14)?

Answer:

The only way the poem can truly be deemed "cubed" is if, while reading it, the poem moves you in some way, whether it's the presence of God, a feeling of inspiration, or a sudden new awareness. That is what gives it the extra dimension, which brings it to life and makes it "cubed."

Illustration:

If you were to take a cube and unfold it—one square up, two squares down, and one square on either side—what do you get? The answer is a *cross*. Behind each cubed poem a bit more of Christ—who died on the cross—is revealed.

Fun Fact:

In Exodus 26, the innermost room of the tabernacle, the Most Holy Place or Holy of Holies—the place where God dwelled, was a cube. And in Revelation 26, "The New Jerusalem"—where God *will* dwell, is also a cube.

Where to Begin

(Laying the Foundation)

Day #1

Love the Lord your God with all your heart and with all your soul and with all your mind and with all your strength.

— Mark 12:30

What Matters Most

Your relationship with God exceeds all else that matters
Without *that*, any other relationship will shatter

What matters next, is preserving your family and your health
 Two aspects many overlook when defining their wealth

Close behind, are friendships, and a passion for what you do
Combined with the above, you cannot be a better you

Aside from what matters, you need to know the things that don't
Though many things may seem to matter, in the end they won't

Money does not matter, apart from providing for needs
Living a lavished life is *not* where the Word of Truth leads

As for appearance and approval, nothing matters less
Such things are no means for measuring how much you are blessed

No possession on earth matters; one day they'll all be gone
Only your relationship with God—**forever**—lives on

How does your life show that you love God with all of your heart, soul, mind, and strength?

Where does God show up on your list of priorities, and why?

What other priorities are competing with your relationship with God?

Try This

Cultivating any meaningful relationship requires time. It's time for a "Reality Check." First list your priorities based on how you spend your time. Make a second list based on how you *should* be spending your time. Then compare the lists and determine how you might make the first fall more in line with the second. Also, be sure to hang the second list in a place you will see and be reminded of daily.

(To download a sample *Reality Check: List of Priorities*, go to EternalThanks.com.)

In answering the first question above, if you love the Lord, you will trust and obey him! Trust and obey God in every area of your life.

Today's Good News

God desires fellowship with you!

Day #2

Now faith is being sure of what we hope for and certain of what we do not see. And without faith it is impossible to please God, because anyone who comes to Him must believe that He exists and that He rewards those who earnestly seek Him.

— **Hebrews 11:1, 6**

Faith

Whether you wish that you may, or wish that you might
No one is perfect, and no one is always right

Part of being human means mistakes will be made
Failure will be found, and at times one's faith may fade

Sooner or later, everyone asks: Is God *real*?
Why can I not see Him? How does having faith *feel*?

Having faith is looking past the pains of today
When all seems lost, *having faith* means you will not stray

It hears what can't be heard, and sees what can't be seen
Faith follows the Living Word—Christ, the Nazarene

Many things occur that are beyond your control
But know: **the strength of your faith... tells how far you'll go**

How can you be sure God exists and rewards those who seek Him?

What things might be weakening your faith?

What are some ways you could strengthen your faith?

Try This

Although wind cannot be seen—it can be felt, and we know that it's there. God is the same way.

Dive into God's Word and pull out 3-5 Bible verses that most inspire you and bring you hope. Write out and memorize these verses so you can refer back to them whenever you may be faltering in your faith. Etch them on your heart. Burn them into your mind. Keep them with you at all times.

(To download a list of *Bible Verse Favorites*, go to EternalThanks.com.)

Also, read (or watch the DVD) *The Case for Faith*, by Lee Strobel.

Today's Good News

God exists and rewards those who seek Him!

Day #3

Whoever wants to save his life will lose it, but whoever loses his life for Me and for the Gospel will save it.

— Mark 8:35

The Meaning of Life

To some, what I'm going to say may sound funny
Life means more than just making a bunch of money

Life means more than having a cool car and huge house
There's more out there than Disney World, and Mickey Mouse

There's much more to this life than how much you possess
There's even more than having good health, and success

If you're thinking: What more can there possibly be?
It's time you look at your life a bit more closely

To learn life's true meaning—to see the big picture
All that you need to know is written in Scripture

Seek Jesus, and listen to what He has to say:
Life's meaning is found, by giving your life away

What brings meaning or significance to *your* life?

How can you bring more meaning to the lives of those around you?

How often do you consult the Bible for guidance and instruction?

Try This

God's Word is meant to be read, and it's to be read daily! Commit to reading the entire Bible in one year, and start *today*. Set aside a specific time each day—for example, in the morning from 7 to 7:15 a.m. Pick a time that works consistently for you. Also, don't just read to get through it; study it. Take note of what God says about how to live. Before each reading, ask God to reveal to you His Son.

(For suggested Bible reading plans, go to HeartLight.org/devotionals/reading_plans.)

If you are not currently involved in a weekly Bible study, consider joining one. Bible Study Fellowship International (BSF) is great! Visit BSFinternational.org to find a class in your area.

Today's Good News

Your life has meaning; you were born for a purpose!

Day #4

...Be made new in the attitude of your minds.

— Ephesians 4:23

Choosing' to' Change

Is there a bad habit or behavior you wish to quit?
Can you see quitting's benefit, yet you still can't commit?

Quitting is never easy; it's a process with a plan
To quit successfully, here's what you need to understand

Most everyone would like to change an aspect of their life
But without Christ, you can't change that which truly causes strife

And though many will say, "*I'll change, someday...*" most never do
For they have not asked Jesus for a mind that's been made new

Breaking a habit is hard, and addictions are the worst
To stop any such cycle, one's *attitude* must change first

It may not seem as though, but you control what's on your mind
The kinds of thoughts you think, lead to the attitude you find

Once the attitude has changed, quitting's process can begin
But where it starts, is asking God, to change you from within

What in your life needs to change?

How will this change improve your life?

What thoughts are holding you back, and how will you overcome them?

Try This

As author Matthew Kelly once so perfectly put it, "Our lives change when our habits change."

Make a list of habits, behaviors, or attitudes you wish to change. Then choose one at a time to focus on, and ask the Holy Spirit to empower you to make that change. Remember: Any major change like this requires planning on your part. Any major change like this requires a plan of action and help from God.

Today's Good News

It's never too late to change!

Day #5

*Do not conform any longer to the pattern of this world, but be
transformed by the renewing of your mind. Then you will
be able to test and approve what God's will is—
His good, pleasing and perfect will.*

— **Romans 12:2**

Transformation

To be transformed—to be made new
Seek God's guidance in all you do

For God's grand plan, is set in stone
So pray *His* will... becomes your own

Unless indeed you are deranged
Don't dwell on what you cannot change

Dwell only on the things you can
Accept all else as God's grand plan

How are you conforming to the patterns of this world?

What in your life needs transformation? What are you doing that is not in line with God's will?

How is God currently transforming you?

Try This

Each morning, before you get out of bed, say this short prayer:

"God, allow me to know and do Your will today, and help me to help others to do the same. Breathe Your life into me, Lord. Transform me into the image of Your Son."

Today's Good News

God has a plan for your life; you are a part of God's grand plan!

Eternal Thanks

(Recognizing Your Blessings)

Day #6

Ears that hear and eyes that see—the Lord has made them both.

— Proverbs 20:12

Coming to Your Senses

Have you ever really wondered how fortunate you are?
Have you ever thought your blessings could outnumber the stars?

First, imagine if you suddenly lost your sense of **sight**
Would you miss seeing the differences, between day and night?

Now imagine if you lost the ability to **hear**
As silence whispers in both ears, could you still persevere?

Now imagine if you suddenly lost your sense of **smell**
Could you bid the sweet scent of flowers and fresh air farewell?

Now imagine if you lost the ability to **taste**
What joy could come from eating, if all flavors were erased?

Now imagine if you suddenly lost your sense of **touch**
Does just the thought, of such a loss, make you *feel* very much?

But since you're blessed with *more* than ears to hear and eyes to see...
Have the sense to thank God... for giving no less than you need

How often do you thank God for all He has given you?

How might you be taking these gifts for granted?

How might you use these gifts to help others?

Try This

Those who are grateful for the things they have are less likely to grumble and complain about the things they don't; it's called having an attitude of gratitude. Create a "List of Gratitude." Write down 20 things you are most grateful for, and hang it somewhere you will see and be reminded of daily.

(To download the *List of Gratitude* template and sample, go to EternalThanks.com.)

Here's another exercise to try: Take a moment and think hard about everything that you have—every possession, every relationship. After you have given it some serious thought, imagine if you suddenly lost it all—everything! It helps to appreciate what you have.

Today's Good News

God never provides less than you need!

Day #7

Give thanks in all circumstances, for this is God's will for you in Christ Jesus.

— 1 Thessalonians 5:18

How Bad Could It Be?

Can questions alone lead to a more thankful attitude?
What could be asked, to improve your own lack of gratitude?

Have you ever been homeless and forced to live on the street?
Have you ever had to dig through garbage for food to eat?

Were you born into poverty, and abused as a child?
Did you grow up never knowing what it felt like to smile?

Do you know what it's like... to bathe in polluted water?
Or to witness the slaughter, of your own son or daughter?

Have you ever been abandoned, by your very own mom?
Have you ever sat six inches from an exploding bomb?

Have you ever been shot, stabbed, tortured, or beaten to death?
How do you think it feels... to know you're breathing your *last* breath?

Will you take to heart, the message, these questions have expressed?
Can you now see—*unquestionably*—how truly you're blessed?

For what do you have to be thankful?

In what ways have you suffered, and what blessings do you see in hindsight?

How can you establish a habit of gratitude?

Try This

To remain grateful for all that we've been given—which is all that we have—we must keep our blessings on the forefront of our minds. Gratefulness must become a daily practice. Begin an "Eternal Journal." Each morning, journal at least 3 new things you are grateful for.

From now on, rather than viewing the glass as "half-empty" or "half-full," be thankful you have a glass at all. Remember, regardless of how bad you think things might be, literally millions of people all around the world would absolutely love to trade places with you.

Today's Good News

You have things to be thankful for; you are truly blessed!

Day #8

...God so loved the world that He gave His one and only Son, that whoever believes in Him shall not perish but have eternal life. For God did not send His Son into the world to condemn the world, but to save the world through Him. Whoever believes in Him is not condemned...

— John 3:16–18

Rude Awakening

Have you ever given the afterlife serious thought?
One day you'll die and be judged, whether you like it or not

On that day, you'll ascend to Heaven, or be sent to Hell
Those are your two options, so know them now, and know them well

Heaven consists of eternal bliss—the best place to go
Hell, there's no place worse than this—it's a blazing inferno

Though most would rather not think about death before they die
If you're to go to Heaven, you must learn how to... and why

Heaven is reserved, for those whom Jesus prepares a place
It's never deserved—it's a gift, given by God through grace

Since Adam and Eve, God sees us as sinfully unclean
We would all call Hell home, had His one Son not intervened

But since Christ died on the cross, to relieve us of our sin
Heaven's gate has flung open... letting all who believe in

How would it feel to be crucified? What do you think would hurt most?

How have you thanked Jesus for the sacrifice He made?

What does Jesus' death say about His love for you?

Try This

Jesus died a most excruciating death, but He *chose* to die. He gave up His life. He died for you, and He died for me.

Watch the film *The Passion of the Christ* (2004). As you are watching, pay close attention to exactly what Jesus went through and imagine how He must have felt. Afterward, say a short prayer thanking Jesus for all that He has done.

Today's Good News

Jesus loves you!

Day #9

*Remember those in prison as if you were their fellow prisoners,
and those who are mistreated as if you yourselves were suffering.*

— Hebrews 13:3

Someone Else's Shoes

How many different pairs of shoes do you have and don't wear?
To the rest of the world, how do you think your shoes compare?

How do they feel? Are they comfortable, or tattered and worn?
More than you'd think, the answer depends on where you were born

If you're one of the fortunate few—you will have many
But the truth of the matter is that *most* don't have any

How do you think it feels to have no shelter for your feet?
How long could you survive on the street, with no food to eat?

Although these thoughts are not pleasant, they mustn't be ignored
For you'll find a thing of beauty, when such thoughts are explored

It's the art of putting yourself in someone else's shoes
A path to empathy, gratitude, and renewed values

If you care for others, and want that concern to be shown
It's time for you to put on someone's shoes besides your own

How often do you think about and pray for those suffering?

How often do you honestly try to put yourself in their shoes?

How does others' suffering put some of your problems into perspective?

Try This

Suffering is an unavoidable aspect of life. Whether you are aware of it or not, there are people all around you who are suffering. Everyone suffers from time to time.

Start praying for those people. Begin seeing things from *their* perspective. Start seeing yourself less and others more. When someone treats you with injustice, for example, ask yourself, "How might that person be suffering?" Then pray that person finds peace. Pray that person finds God.

Today's Good News

You can be a blessing to those who are suffering!

Day #10

This is the day the Lord has made; let us rejoice and be glad in it.

— Psalms 118:24

The Best Day Ever

How would you like each new day to be the best day ever?
Would it be worth taking on a tough mental endeavor?

Would it be worth letting go, of anxiety and grief?
Would it be worth such a joy, as everlasting relief?

What makes one day entirely better than all the rest?
What is it that makes one day, particularly, *the best*?

You'll be glad to know it calls for no divine provision
All it takes, is for you to make a conscious decision

To not let weather or circumstance control how you feel
To anticipate the good that comes from every ordeal

To hold an eternal perspective firmly in both hands
And accept all things as being part of God's perfect plan

It's perception that determines the outcome of your day
Keep this in mind, at all times, and you'll be well on your way

How are you rejoicing and being glad this day?

How would you describe the best day ever?

What does it mean to have an eternal perspective?

Try This

Each new day has the potential to be the best day ever! But it's completely up to you.

Before getting out of bed for the day, say this: "*I* control what I think about and how I will respond to things; therefore, *I* control how I feel. Today is going to be the best day ever!" Make the conscious decision to let this day be the best day ever.

Then tomorrow do it all over again... and again... and then again.

Today's Good News

Each new day can be the best day ever!

Trials & Triumphs

(Acknowledging & Overcoming Obstacles)

Day #11

Do not be anxious about anything, but in everything, by prayer and petition, with thanksgiving, present your requests to God. And the peace of God, which transcends all understanding, will guard your hearts and your minds in Christ Jesus.

— Philippians 4:6–7

Freedom from Fear

Try to understand what needs to be understood
Worrying does not do anyone any good

In order for your worries to be whisked away
Pray... and accept tomorrow before it's today

For whatever has happened, cannot be undone
And all that is to come, is known by only One

So don't fear the future—whatever it may bring
Just be prepared to not anticipate a thing

Request the Peace of God to guard your heart and mind
Allow Him to let you leave your worries behind

From the bondage of all fear and anxiety
God is here—willing and able to set you free

What are you worrying about? What do you fear?

What good have you found that comes from worrying?

Why should you present your requests and release your worries to God?

Try This

There are two types of worries:

1. That which you can do something about.
2. That which you have no control over.

Make a list of all your worries. Identify that which you can do something about; then decide possible plans of action. As for what's left, take a deep breath; as you exhale, pray for God to take those worries away (read off each item and, as it leaves your lips, release it to God). When finished, crumple up or shred apart the list, and throw it away.

(To download a *Worry Release Sheet*, go to EternalThanks.com.)

Next time you feel overly anxious, repeat the above steps.

Today's Good News

You can have freedom from fear!

Day #12

Watch out! Be on your guard against all kinds of greed; a man's life does not consist in the abundance of his possessions.

— Luke 12:15

Contentment vs. Greed

Tell me why, as fortunate as we are
Our satisfaction only goes so far

We tend to want more and more... and then MORE
If it's never enough, what's it good for?

It's a case of Contentment vs. Greed
Can we not live without what we don't need?

Can't we just be grateful that we're alive?
Or are we *content* letting *greed* survive?

If you love life, and truly want to live
Rid yourself of greed, and learn how to give

In what areas of your life do you lack contentment?

How are you guarding yourself against all kinds of greed?

How could you give more to others (or back to God)?

Try This

The cure for greed is giving... habitually.

Start setting aside a portion of your income so that when the opportunity presents itself, you can give. Perhaps give a percentage of your income to a charity (or charities) of your choice—consider sponsoring a child (Compassion.com). This discipline not only helps others, but it keeps greed at bay. Remember, giving is meant to be a joy, not a pain.

It doesn't take a whole lot to give. From a kind word, to returning a smile, practice giving this week. You can even give (of your time) by praying for someone. Keep in mind that giving does not have to involve money.

Today's Good News

You have something to offer; you have something to give!

Day #13

I can do everything through Him who gives me strength.

— Philippians 4:13

Inspiration

Ever felt like you've completely lost your motivation?
Where does one begin to look, to find new inspiration?

Well, when's the last time you took an honest look at your dreams?
The odds are, the time since last, has been longer than it seems

For we're driven by our dreams—our inner most desires
The way we wish things could be! *That's* what ever inspires

Stop letting perfectly good motivation go to waste
It's time that you realize: **your dreams are meant to be chased**

So gather each of your dreams, and write them all down—right now!
Do not lose sight of them again; make this a solemn vow

Share them with others; don't be scared to let the whole world know
Then all that's left to do, is convert those dreams into goals

What do you wish to accomplish? Where would you like to be?
What's the single, most important thing you hope to achieve?

What are you passionate about?

What (or who) is keeping you from pursuing your dreams?

What (or who) is the source of your strength?

Try This

Dreams drive us! But to be driven by our dreams, we must be in touch with our dreams. So, start a dream journal.

Begin by jotting down your "Top 10 Dreams" (things you wish to accomplish, become, or do), and don't hold back! If you want to travel the world or run a marathon, write it down. Let your imagination run wild! As soon as you're done, share those dreams with someone you trust will encourage you—then hang the list up in a place you will glance at daily. And be sure to revisit your dream journal often.

(To download a *Top 10 Dreams* template, go to EternalThanks.com.)

Remember, you *can* do everything through Him who gives you strength, including accomplishing goals and achieving your dreams.

Today's Good News

It's never too late to pursue your dreams!

Day #14

Come to Me, all you who are weary and burdened,
and I will give you rest...

— **Matthew 11:28**

Finding the Strength to Sleep

Have you ever been unable to find the strength to sleep?
Although you're truly tired, the exhaustion runs too deep

At first, everything seems normal, as the minutes pass by
But for some strange reason—you *can't* sleep, and you don't know why

Lying in bed, your thoughts slowly move faster and faster
Then anxiety hits you—like a sudden disaster

In complete darkness, the world begins to spin around you
You wish to make it stop, but you have no clue what to do

Like a frightened, upset child, you sit up, tremble, and shake
"What is going on? What is it that's keeping me awake!"

You may feel lost and alone, but the truth is that you're not
The solution is right there... He simply needs to be sought

If ever lost in your thoughts, you must remember to pray
For the Father is waiting, to take your worries away

What is keeping *you* up at night? What burdens do you bear?

How often do you seek out Jesus for rest?

How often do you talk with God? How often do you pray?

Try This

Praying and growing closer to God go hand in hand. And praying is nothing more than talking with God.

Make prayer a daily practice. Pray when you get up; pray before each meal; and pray when you go to bed. Continue to talk with God more and more each day until you are in continuous prayer, bringing everything to Him. Possible points to include in each prayer: **ACTS**

A - Adoration - praise God for who He is.
C - Confession - own up to your sins.
T - Thanksgiving - thank God for all He has done.
S - Supplication - make requests for others and yourself.

Today's Good News

God is never more than a prayer away!

Day #15

...Jesus said, "If you hold to My teaching, you are really My disciples. Then you will know the truth, and the truth will set you free."

— John 8:31–32

Defeating Depression

Have you ever been entirely filled with emptiness?
Has your soul, been a black hole—void of hope and happiness?

Whether it's a disease or disorder, what can you do?
Besides sin, where can you turn to fill that void within you?

In a state of depression, is a sad, sad place to be
When you don't feel like living, can the truth still set you free?

Can it sober up the face that sleeps on filthy old rugs?
Can it pull you out from under the influence of drugs?

Can it release you from the grips of your worst addiction?
Is it able to turn disbelief—into conviction?

If you're in that sad, sad place... and you don't feel you can cope
It's time you turn to the only source that can bring you hope

No challenge is ever impossible to rise above
When you fix your eyes upon the Light, and the Truth... God's love

How are you holding to Jesus' teaching?

Who are some people you can turn to when feeling sad or depressed?

How often do you fix your eyes on the Light, which is the Truth, which is God's love?

Try This

The truth is, everyone gets depressed from time to time. In a quiet place with no distractions—for at least one minute a day—close your eyes and meditate on nothing but God and His love for you. Empty your mind of all thoughts and concerns; just be present to God's presence and remain still. Set a timer if it helps, but don't look at it. See how much of a difference just one minute a day can make!

Also, listen to the three-part Focus on the Family radio broadcast *Depression: Encouragement for the Journey*, by Reverend Tommy Nelson. Here's a man who's been through it, and lived to tell about it.

(FocusOnTheFamily.com is a wellspring of practical, godly advice.)

Today's Good News

You are loved; God loves you so much!

At the Heart of It All

(Receiving Christ)

Day #16

Jesus answered, "I am the way, the truth, and the life. No one comes to the Father, except through Me."

— John 14:6

The Good News

What I hold is more valuable than anything on earth
A piece of knowledge, with an unimaginable worth

It's a precious message, of forgiveness, mercy, and grace
The truths—about God, sin, Christ, and man—I pray you embrace

Please do not take offense to this, and *know* it's no story
God gives us all life, but we all fall short of His glory

By not following His commands, we chose to misbehave
Now, far from God man stands—desperately needing to be saved

But there's good news, for those who repent and choose to believe
In Christ, God promises salvation for all to receive

To atone for the world's sin, He paid the ultimate price
God gave His one Son, His own life—the greatest sacrifice

With His last breath, Christ conquered sin and death... He rose again
Jesus is the **Truth**, the **Life**, and the **Only Way**... Amen!

What is your response to the Gospel?

What ways other than Jesus are you trying to get into Heaven?

How are you following Jesus?

Try This

Accepting and declaring Christ as your savior is the single, most important decision you will ever make.

It is also important to know why you believe what you believe and have solid evidence to back it up. Read (or watch the DVD) *The Case for Christ*, by Lee Strobel and *Surprised by Faith*, by Dr. Don Bierle. Both are great books on the subject.

Also, as soon as you get a chance, check out NeedHim.com. This website does a wonderful job of introducing others to Christ.

Today's Good News

Jesus broke down all barriers between you and God!

Life in Christ

(Committing Your Life to Christ)

Day #17

...If you confess with your mouth, "Jesus is Lord," and believe in your heart that God raised Him from the dead, you will be saved.

— **Romans 10:9**

Salvation

In this world of uncertainty, how can you be sure you are saved?
What guarantee do you have sin's penalty has truly been paid?

If you research the subject for yourself, you will see that it's true
You can trust in the Bible—it is reliable, through and through

It's packed with fulfilled prophecies and historical evidence
Therefore, it takes no leap of faith for belief in its relevance

It says we've all missed the mark because of our sinful behavior
It says Jesus Christ, sacrificed His life, to become our Savior

It says Christ took our place on the cross, yet God raised Him from the dead
It says unbelievers began believing, thus the Gospel spread

From generation to generation—throughout every nation
The curse of condemnation, became reversed into salvation

God's gift of deliverance, has since been presented to receive
All it takes is for your mouth to confess, and your heart to believe

"Jesus **is** my Lord and Savior, and God **did** raise Him from the dead!"
With that being said, go into the world, and let salvation spread

What does your mouth confess, and what does your heart believe?

Whom do you know who has yet to be saved?

How are you spreading the message of salvation?

Try This

It's hard to spread a message you yourself have questions about. If you have any questions regarding your faith—any questions at all, go to GotQuestions.org.

It's okay to have doubts. In this life, you will never have *all* the answers. What is important about faith though, is that, in spite of doubt, you press forward—continually pursuing God.

Also, be sure to read the book or listen to the audio version of *Mere Christianity*, by C.S. Lewis. With thoughts as deep as his logic, you are sure to gain new insights on the matter.

Lastly, watch Rob Bell's *Everything Is Spiritual* on DVD. Few sermons are as educational and entertaining as this.

Today's Good News
Salvation is God's gift to you, and it's free!

Day #18

Enter through the narrow gate. For wide is the gate and broad is the road that leads to destruction, and many enter through it. But small is the gate and narrow the road that leads to life, and only a few find it.

— Matthew 7:13–14

The Narrow Road

It's a matter of **LIFE** or *death*—**SPIRIT** or *flesh*; you choose
The Bible bestows guidance you can follow or refuse

It tells of two separate roads, which lead to two separate gates
Two alternative entries, to two alternative fates

What awaits is genuine faith, or worldly demise
To avoid the latter, the right road must be recognized

One is ever so narrow; the other, extremely wide
The first is paved with humility; the second with pride

The first stares each evil, wicked desire in the face
It rests in God's promises, and is grateful for His grace

The second flees from truth, and is a whole different story
It cares more for self-indulgence, than God and His glory

Jesus says, "*Enter through the narrow gate that's found by few.*"
Whether you follow Christ's direction... that's left up to you

How are you following Christ's direction?

What road are you on right now?

What obstacles might you expect to face while traveling the narrow road?

Try This

To live by the Spirit, as opposed to by the flesh, is a struggle fought daily within us all. The narrow road (or higher ground) is a path paved with humility. As Zig Ziglar once put it, "Humility is not thinking less of yourself; it's thinking of yourself less."

For a captivating depiction of one's journey traveling the narrow road, read *The Pilgrim's Progress* (in Modern English), by John Bunyan. It's been called by some "the greatest allegory ever written."

Lastly, pray for a humble heart. Ask Jesus to literally live through you; ask Him to guide your thoughts and actions. Give Him control of your body and mind—surrender yourself fully—and let Him direct you in love. Try seeing things through *His* eyes, and be amazed by what you see.

Today's Good News

You can choose life; you can walk with Jesus!

Day #19

...Whatever you do, do it all for the glory of God.

— 1 Corinthians 10:31

The Holy Trail

How would you like to live a life beyond your wildest dreams?
To open up your eyes and see what living truly means?

Would you like to find the Holy Grail and Fountain of Youth?
Then follow Jesus' trail: the Way to a Life of Truth

For it's not about gaining or obtaining worldly things
It's not about singing and dancing and living as kings

It's to commit and submit yourself fully to His will
It's being present to His presence, and remaining still

Do not look down on others; help them to look up instead
Be grateful and thankful, and always share your daily bread

Be selective and wise—with how and whom you spend your time
Gladly greet each mountain of challenge... and enjoy the climb!

In truth, it's better that you never find fortune and fame
To live is to know your maker, and magnify **His Name**

How much time do you spend each day pursuing spiritual things?

Where could you be more selective with how and whom you spend your time?

How well do you know God? How often do you magnify His name?

Try This

God deserves 100% of the honor, glory, and praise. Our main purpose on earth is to glorify God; however, this is not our normal inclination. We are much more inclined to do the opposite, which is glorifying ourselves (or someone or something else).

Make a list of at least 10 practical ways you could glorify *His* name. Throughout the week, do 3 or more of the things on that list. Be intentional about it. Plan out how and when you will do them—actually write them into your schedule. Try doing this until glorifying God becomes second nature.

(To view or download *30 Practical Ways to Glorify God*, go to EternalThanks.com.)

Today's Good News

You can know God!

Day #20

...Faith by itself, if it is not accompanied by action, is dead.

— James 2:17

Faith in Action

It's tough to battle notions others preconceive
But that's no reason not to say what you believe

Yet there's not a lot to say that hasn't been said
So forget about talking—take action instead!

Take hold of hypocrisy, and tear it apart
Love each of your enemies, with all of your heart

Forgive any trespass—future, past, or present
Bear others' burdens, no matter how unpleasant

Welcome the least and lost to feast at your table
Give gladly to the poor, as much as you're able

Let go of the wheel; let the Holy Spirit drive
Through all your actions, show that Jesus is alive!

How are you acting on your faith?

What role does hypocrisy play in your life? How are you not practicing what you preach?

What actions show others that Jesus lives in you?

Try This

Faith without action is no faith at all. Nothing proves one's faith better than one's actions; so put your faith into action. Do something! Act on your faith! Read *Don't Waste Your Life*, by John Piper, and pray for God to reveal new ways to put your faith into action.

Begin asking yourself what the motive or main driving force is behind each of your actions. Are you doing it out of love, for God, or something else?

Today's Good News

You have the ability to act on your faith!

Day #21

Let the peace of Christ rule in your heart...

— Colossians 3:15

Peace on Earth

For most people, the idea of *peace on earth* does not exist
It's become a happy afterthought most have happily dismissed

"Who cares about peace, when there's money to make, and power to gain?"
Sadly, this worldly pursuit, has made many humans inhumane

Hearts of many have become colder than ice, and harder than rock
Never skipping a beat: E-vil-Cau-ses-Cha-os-A-round-the-clock

Is peace on earth even possible, or an immense waste of time?
It's hard to imagine, when all that's seen is violence, war, and crime

Even so, peace on earth would still be great, that much can't be denied
But the world's not willing to take up its cross, or be crucified

It would rather have people believe that peace has been forbidden
Yet the truth of the matter is that peace has just been well hidden

Inside every soul, just beneath the guilt and shame that comes with sin
It's waiting... and fills the hearts of all those who choose to let Christ in

If you want to find peace on earth, there are three things you need to do
Grab hold of Jesus, let go of sin, and allow peace to find *you*

How does sin keep you from experiencing peace through Jesus?

When are you letting the peace of Christ rule in your heart?

Where and how could you promote peace on earth?

Try This

Peace is not just the absence of conflict, but a wholeness that can come only from God. Peace is one of the great fruits of the Spirit.

Begin to become conscious of your breathing. Start by taking a few deep breaths in and out. As you inhale, imagine your body being filled with the Spirit of Jesus and His eternal peace. As you exhale, imagine your body being emptied of every worry and concern. Breathe in peace and Christ; breathe out worry and fear. Practice this exercise often.

Today's Good News

God can make you whole; God can bring you peace!

Characteristics of Christ

(Living in His Likeness)

Day #22

...The fruit of the Spirit is love, joy, peace, patience, kindness, goodness, faithfulness, gentleness, and self-control.

— Galatians 5:22–23

Fruit of the Spirit

When you meet a true Christian, what qualities do you see?
Hopefully, a reverence for God, that's shown most **joyfully**

By examples they set—like giving not to get, they lead
With such **kindness** and **peace**, they **gently** help others in need

As much as for themselves, they show a **love** for their neighbor
And through **goodness** and **patience**, they seek to thrill their Savior

Showing thanks, they are grateful for every gift they receive
And by the sharing of their **faith**, others come to believe

In Jesus' name, they maintain **self-control**, and don't judge
Like Christ, they practice forgiveness, and will not hold a grudge

When times are bad—and become worse, their actions show they care
And each night—before they sleep—for *you* they say a small prayer

While they live to please the heavens, until the bitter end
It's through them, the delicious fruits of the Spirit transcend

What kind of "fruit" are you producing?

Which fruit of the Spirit will you ask God to develop and grow in you?

What do you need to *stop* doing in order to be more like Jesus?

Try This

The fruit of the Spirit only partly describes the character of Christ. To *live* like Jesus, you must *think* like Jesus.

Although now a cliché, before each decision, ask yourself, "*What Would Jesus Do?*" and pray for discernment. It might help to wear a What Would Jesus Do (WWJD) band or bracelet as a reminder. By the way, WWJD also stands for "Walk With Jesus Daily."

Today's Good News

You can make a difference; you can *be* the difference!

Day #23

Then He said to them all: "If anyone would come after Me, he must deny himself and take up his cross daily and follow Me."

— Luke 9:23

Self-DeniaL

Though it's easy to detect, and can be seen from afar
Most people just aren't that mindful of how selfish they are

How frequently do you seek to serve without any gain?
How often do you get your way, and yet you still complain?

How often do you put another's needs before your own?
How seldom is self-denial and self-sacrifice shown?

The truth is, selfishness is quite a common condition
To conquer it, life in Christ must be your main ambition

Do you know how to die to self, and start living for Christ?
God is the *only* power source, that can and will suffice

While supplying you with self-discipline and self-control
His Holy Spirit enables you to tell the flesh, "*No.*"

In all circumstances, look to Jesus that you may see...
What it means to walk in love—and deny yourself daily

What are some actions that reveal your own selfishness?

Where could you use more self-discipline or self-control?

What are some ways you deny yourself, and how often do you do so?

Try This

It is impossible to take up your cross without denying yourself; taking up your cross *is* denying yourself.

Make a conscious effort to deny yourself today. Purposely put someone else's needs before your own. Ask Jesus for the strength to take up your cross and follow Him. And remember, self-denial is not a one-time event; it's an ongoing process.

Today's Good News

You control the flesh; the flesh does not control *you!*

Day #24

...Forgive whatever grievances you may have against one another. Forgive as the Lord forgave you.

— Colossians 3:13

Forgiveness

Forgiveness is a fragile matter that most don't handle with care
All too often it's withheld, and the act has become far too rare

The world we live in is a mercilessly unforgiving place
Where—not only are grudges held, but anger and hate are embraced

The Bible tells us this: **be quick to forgive, as Christ forgave you**
Can you forgive without limit, regardless of what others do?

To "*Live and Let Live*" and "*Forgive and Forget*" sound easy enough
However, to accomplish such a feat, is a whole lot more tough

For to forgive, is to give up your right to be hurt or upset
And that's tricky, when the wrong that's been done is so hard to forget

But to purposely *not* forgive, does you absolutely no good
For such resentment prevents you, from loving others as you should

Don't allow bitterness to weigh you down; let God lighten the load
Let the Spirit move you to show the same forgiveness *Jesus* showed

Once it's forgiveness that's embraced, anger is replaced... with healing
An amazingly freeing, utterly magnificent feeling!

What does God's willingness to forgive mean to you?

How is anger, bitterness, or resentment controlling you?

Whom do you need to forgive?

Try This

Through Christ's death on the cross, His life being the payment for our sins, we are reconciled to God; we are forgiven. All He asks is that we do the same: forgive.

Forgiving is not easy, but, if you want to grow closer to God, it must be done. Forgive from your heart those you have not yet forgiven, including yourself. Remind yourself of how God has forgiven you. Make a list of as many of your own sins and mistakes as you can, and then ask God in prayer to give you a heart to forgive others whom you are reluctant to forgive—just as He has forgiven you.

Today's Good News

You are forgiven; you are reconciled to God!

Day #25

The integrity of the upright guides them, but the unfaithful are destroyed by their duplicity.

— **Proverbs 11:3**

Integrity

In reality, you just might be someone else—to everyone
And playing different roles, around different souls, is not always fun

Around certain people, there are certain things that you must not do
But what is the point of living, if—while living, you can't be you?

Restricting your actions and words for specific people seems wrong
Perhaps that is why *integrity* makes a person *truly* strong

Those who have it, don't worry about disguises to hide behind
And when you look to them, there is but one honest person you'll find

But those who lack integrity, wind up wearing masks of deceit
Their true faces are unknown, rarely shown, as well as incomplete

If that's you, choose to rid yourself of the many masks that you wear
Uncover the true creation that God intended to be there

One guided by conviction that never gives in to compromise
One upheld by faith that falls for none of Satan's soul-taking lies

A beautiful tapestry—like Jesus—hung for the world to see
Woven together, by a life lived in truth... and integrity

How would others describe you? As a person of integrity or something else?

How are you being unfaithful and deceiving others? Where might you be compromising your integrity?

How is integrity guiding you?

Try This

Become your word. Do what you say you are going to do, and hold yourself accountable. As Jesus says, "Simply let your 'Yes' be 'Yes,' and your 'No,' 'No'" (Matthew 5:37).

One way to do this is by writing down a plan each week and following through with it. Pick a night (like Sunday) to sit down and seriously carve out your schedule (it should take about 15-20 minutes). Do this the same night each week until it's a habit. If you don't have a planner, be sure to get one.

(To download your own *Weekly Planner Sheet*, go to EternalThanks.com.)

Today's Good News

You don't have to lie; you can tell the truth!

Day #26

...Let us run with perseverance the race marked out for us. Let us fix our eyes on Jesus, the author and perfecter of our faith, who for the joy set before Him endured the cross... Consider Him who endured such opposition from sinful men, so that you will not grow weary and lose heart.

— **Hebrews 12:1–3**

Perseverance

What makes one decide to go the distance?
Sheer determination, and persistence

Run the race with your eyes fixed on one place
Unto Jesus: perfecter of our faith

For there is nothing that you cannot do
Once you have harnessed Christ's strength within you

Become driven. Do what needs to be done
Every time! —Finish what you have begun

When your only option is to persist
Then—to you—failure no longer exists

How often are your eyes fixed on Jesus?

What distractions are keeping you from doing what needs to be done?

How would your attitude change if you knew you could not fail?

Try This

Jesus Christ is the ultimate example of perseverance. When we fix our eyes on *Him*, and He gives us the strength, nothing is impossible.

Nevertheless, doing what needs to be done is easier to do when what needs to be done is written down. First thing each day (or night before), make a To-Do List consisting of no more than 3-5 major tasks, and prioritize them. Work your way through the list focusing on one task at a time. Do not move on until each task is completed. All the while, keep in mind how it will feel to know you did what needed to be done and you persevered.

(Again, for a *Weekly Planner Sheet*, go to EternalThanks.com.)

Today's Good News

You can do it, and God can help!

Where to Go from Here

(Finishing the Race)

❧❦❧

Day #27

Jesus replied: "'Love the Lord your God with all your heart and with all your soul and with all your mind.' This is the first and greatest commandment. And the second is like it: 'love your neighbor as yourself.'"

— Matthew 22:37–39

How to Love Your Neighbor

"Love your neighbor as you love yourself"; 'tis easier said than done
For we're also told to, above all else, *"Look out for Number One."*

Society tells us one thing, while Jesus tells us another
So what are we to do, follow the masses, or love each other?

What if we *were* to love our neighbors as ourselves? What would that mean?
A lot of things would have to change, starting with how strangers are seen

For neighbors consist of *more* than just the people who live next door
It includes those we choose not to see—those we normally ignore

A neighbor is anyone you know of, in any way in need
Which should be everyone, so how in the world are we to proceed?

To love everyone as yourself, you need to be intentional
Everyday—in everyway—go beyond what's unconventional

Be like Jesus: see each person as a beautiful creation
Seek the Spirit's help, and use your limitless imagination

To show the same love for yourself, to the entire human race
From now on: **picture a mirror in place of every person's face**

How often, and in what ways, do you love your neighbor as yourself?

What kind of example are you setting for others?

Who is in need of your help? Whom might you be overlooking?

Try This

To *love* everyone as yourself, it helps to *see* everyone as yourself.

From now on, as often as you can, imagine a mirror in place of each person's face. Envision everyone you see as a reflection of you. Treat them exactly as you would want them to treat you. And, if possible, try bringing a smile to each of their faces.

The Golden Rule is not dead; we just don't practice it as often as we ought to.

Today's Good News

You can be like Jesus; you can love!

Day #28

Do not let any unwholesome talk come out of your mouths, but only what is helpful for building others up according to their needs, that it may benefit those who listen.

— **Ephesians 4:29**

Gossip into' GospeL

Why is gossip so popular and so easily spread?
Why can't we all be nicer and just share good news instead?

 Hearing others' trials, must take the focus off our own
 That must be why such nonsense is so heavily condoned

"*Gossip*" is sharing other people's personal info
So, its very meaning is "*stuff you're not supposed to know*"

But it can't and won't be stopped, unless it begins with you
Right now—from now on—start thinking things more thoroughly through

Ask, "*What should I do?*" so you need not say, "*What have I done!*"
In every instance, protect your ears and control your tongue

Don't open your mouth unless you're fine with being quoted
Select each word wisely, for they all are being noted

When it comes to what's worth being said, refer to God's Word
Compliments & Encouragement... *that's* what needs to be heard

What unwholesome talk comes out of your mouth?

How could you better guard your ears and control your tongue?

How is your ability to speak benefiting others? How often do you compliment and encourage?

Try This

Words are powerful. Words are more powerful than most people know. They can be used to build up, or to tear down.

Before you speak, ask yourself, "*How might others benefit from what I'm about to say?*" If they are not going to benefit from it, don't say it. Also, make it a habit to compliment and encourage at least two different people each day. Think of something nice to say, and be genuine. Use your words to build others up.

Today's Good News
You have the ability to build others up!

Day #29

...Go into all the world and preach the Good News to all creation.

— Mark 16:15

This Very Moment

A single, solitary moment is all that it will take
It's a short amount of time, but what a difference it can make

Take for instance—right this minute, before long it will be gone
It's quite humbling to consider just how much is going on

This very moment, a mother who's lost her child is crying
This very moment, a boy you don't even know is dying

This very moment, a confused man is cheating on his wife
This very moment, someone's dear friend is taking his own life

This very moment, a young girl is suffering from cancer
This very moment, a dad is praying to God for answers...

The list can go on and on, but the point is simple and true
The world is a big place, and it does *not* revolve around you

Though we all have problems of our own, others' can't be ignored
That's why, besides helping another, there's no greater reward
Whom can you think of—right now—in need, who doesn't know the Lord?

How are you spreading the Good News to all creation?

How often are you present to the moment (or present *in* the moment)?

Whom do you know personally who doesn't know Jesus?

Try This

Sometimes all it takes to witness for Christ is sharing your story, and nobody knows your story better than you.

Create your own "Personal Faith Story." After you are done, share it with someone. Include one paragraph for each of the following:

1. Your life before Jesus Christ

2. How you came to Christ

3. What Jesus has done in your life

4. What Jesus is doing in your life now

(To download or view a *Personal Faith Story* template and sample, go to EternalThanks.com.)

Today's Good News

You can change people's lives; your story is worth sharing!

Day #30

Therefore, my dear brothers, stand firm. Let nothing move you. Always give yourselves fully to the work of the Lord, because you know that your labor in the Lord is not in vain.

— 1 Corinthians 15:58

Delayed Gratification

Here's a concept that's foreign—to almost all kids and adults
Actions taken NOW, don't always see immediate results

In truth, most things worth working toward, take time to be realized
Or else hard work would not exist, so take note—and be advised

A firm foundation must first be built, before it all begins
And focus must be found, even as the world around you spins

If you do as Jesus did, you can persist past any pain
If you learn to stand firm, knowing your labor is not in vain

Effort is never wasted simply because you don't get paid
Try to understand: **gratification... is at times delayed**

It can come in many forms, and it can come in many ways
It can come when least expected, so don't sit and count the days

But while you're waiting, be sure to always give your very best
In all things, be patient, and know that God's glory is professed
And never delay your gratitude, for being truly blessed

How can you fully give yourself to the work of the Lord, and how often do you do so?

In what areas do you need to "stand firm"—letting nothing move you?

In what ways can delayed gratification be a blessing?

Try This

In one more day you will be finished reading this book. If this is your first time, as soon as you are done, start over. This time answer each question and complete as many action steps as you can before moving on. Just as faith without works is dead, knowledge without application is worthless.

Remember, each action is meant to build upon your relationship with God and bring you closer to Him. It will take longer, but that's what delayed gratification is all about: standing firm and pushing onward regardless of how long it takes. It's a struggle, but in the end it's worth it!

Today's Good News

Your labor is not in vain; your eternal reward is yet to come!

Day #31

*This is how we know what love is: Jesus Christ laid down
His life for us...*

— 1 John 3:16

Hope

Society today is a mixture of race and religion
Where fists fly in the form of voices, pushing their own opinion

Stereotypes continue leading people to poorly misjudge
While ignorance is reinforced, with a stubbornness that won't budge

With countless different points of view causing misinterpretation
Where one problem lies, is in finding improved communication

Communication is a two-way street, where traffic moves both ways
Learn to listen before you speak; observe what others have to say

If you don't agree, don't argue; respectfully state your own claim
Everyone is different, so the way we all think *won't* be the same

All thoughts, feelings, and beliefs, can never be forced to fall in line
That's part of what makes—so special—God's awesomely flawless design

He does not ask that you try to change the opinion of others
Your only task: love each person, like a *true* sister or brother

Despite any difference found, know this and hope will never be lost
We do share a common ground: **Jesus died for us all on the cross.**

Besides Jesus, how many people have laid down their life for you?

Whose opinion are you trying to change, and how are you going about it?

What gives you hope, and how do you provide hope for others?

Try This

Intercessory prayer is a more than mighty tool.

Create a list of "People to Pray For." List everyone you can think of (family, friends, *enemies*, etc.). Then, each night before bedtime, read the list. As you say each name, think about that individual—picture their face, imagine their trials, and ask God to give them hope.

(To download a *People to Pray For* template, go to EternalThanks.com.)

Note: If you do not plan on reading this book again anytime soon, instead of having it collect dust on a shelf somewhere, please pass it on to someone else who might benefit from reading it.

Today's Good News

You don't ever have to lose hope... ever again!

The Importance of Repetition

Although some messages are so powerful they can instantly change a person's view on things forever, that is not normally the case. What usually happens is the person is inspired for a day or two and then the message itself slowly fades away. As the old saying goes, "Out of sight, out of mind."

How often have you heard a great message and come next week—or the next day even—you can't even remember what the sermon was about? It happens all the time! That is why it is so important to take notes during church. For a great message to have any lasting impact, it must be revisited regularly. If you take notes, the notes are what allow you to revisit and absorb the message. It's just like learning a new skill: repetition is key. As Zig Ziglar says, "Repetition is the mother of learning, the father of action, and the architect of accomplishment." Again, repetition is key.

Hanging biblically based poetry on the wall serves as another catalyst for repetition. It's not just there to look pretty; it's there to inspire. More than decoration, it's life transformation! When its message is seen and read every single day, *it has an effect on you*. Like a faucet slowly dripping water onto a giant sponge, every time a pair of eyes gazes upon its frame and reads the words within, a bit more of the message is absorbed.

Another great catalyst for repetition is the habit of reading a devotional book each day, more specifically: each morning. The best way to start the day—besides reading directly from the Bible—is reading a daily devotional (like this one) that has messages from the Bible in it. I highly recommend *My Utmost for His Highest*, by Oswald Chambers. Flicking the "on" switch to the brain, devotionals give the mind worthwhile things to think about. Most always, as you close the book, you are left with a positive outlook, which—if you so choose—can easily be carried throughout the rest of the day.

So, take notes in church. Hang inspirational messages on the wall. Read daily devotional books. And don't forget: *Repetition is Key.*

Final Thoughts

Dear Reader,

Thank you so much for reading this book. I hope you have enjoyed reading it as much as I have enjoyed writing it!

When I first felt God calling me to write "cubed" poetry, I had a vision. I envisioned these poems being hung up on countless walls in churches and homes across the country. I envisioned these poems serving as a daily reminder of God's presence and His love for us. That is why, today, each one of the poems in this book hangs on my bedroom wall. And they do just that; they remind me of God's presence and His love for me.

If any of the poems in *Good News for a Month* have encouraged you and you would like to see it daily or perhaps share it with someone as a gift, please visit *EternalThanks.com*. A uniquely framed version of each poem along with its verse of Scripture is available to purchase.

To God be the glory!

Yours in Christ,

J. Arthur Teresi

Acknowledgments

Gratitude begins with giving thanks. When I think about the evolution and shaping of this book, a few specific people come to mind:

Jesus Christ, thank you... for everything.

Heather Christian, thank you for your encouragement and thoughtfulness.

Heather Prestegord, thank you for the positive feedback and insightful ideas.

Tom & Jeanne Ibach, thank you for sifting through the content of each page. The numerous suggestions you offered had a more than noticeable effect.

Greg Lowery, thank you for meeting with me on more than one occasion and pushing me out of my comfort zone. Your ideas were invaluable.

Evan Brue, thank you for your suggestions and insights. Fellowship with you and your family has been an enormous blessing and encouragement.

Brian Teresi, thank you for being my editor. You are great at pointing out my mistakes, but even better at offering constructive criticism.

Harvey Rothman, Katie Hochstaetter, and Cindy Benzaquen, thank you for your artistic brilliance. The illustrations for cover ideas were amazing.

Nic Westlake, thank you for the countless hours you spent giving this book, the website, and the framed poems their phenomenal look. You did a fantastic job.

Brandon Cernoch and Marcus Montana, thank you for being excellent examples of what it means to be a brother in Christ.

And lastly, I would like to thank my family members who have always believed in me: Mike Teresi, Cindy & Momy Benzaquen, Norma MacDonald, Julie Christian, Barb & Tom Teresi, DeeDee & Chuck Bolter (God rest his soul), Steve Teresi, Nia, Brandi, Jordan, Hunter, and Rylee.

I am extremely grateful to have each one of you in my life. Thank you all!

For more information, or to contact J. Arthur

Visit EternalThanks.com

⳾ternal thanks

Bringing Gratitude to Life

❧❦❧

Inspirational | Motivational | Devotional